Step by Ste

Noah's Ark

Leena Lane and Gillian Chapman

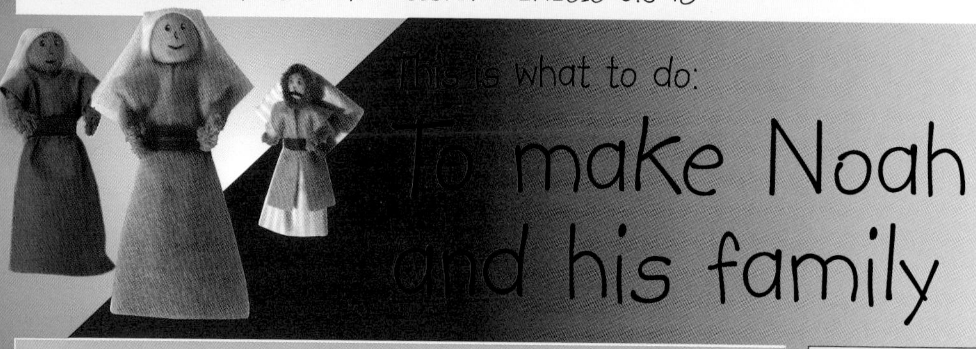

This is what to do:

To make Noah and his family

Here's the story of one good man
in a world that was sad and grim.
His name was Noah, he trusted God,
and that's why God saved him.
A flood was coming to cover the lands,
but Noah and his sons were in God's
safe hands.

You will need:

- Small wooden beads, 18mm long
- Long 'craft' pipe cleaners
- Permanent ink black felt tipped pen
- Scraps of felt and fabric
- Thin card
- Yarn
- PVA glue in bottle with nozzle
- Small stick for Noah
- Sticky tape
- Scissors
- Ruler

To make Noah

1. Bend a pipe cleaner in half to make the body.
2. Push a second pipe cleaner through the two halves to make the arms.
3. Twist the first pipe cleaner to secure the arms in place.
4. Fold each arm to meet the body and twist.
5. Glue a small bead on to the neck to make the head.
6. Wind coloured yarn around the arms to cover the pipe cleaners, knotting the ends together or tucking them under and gluing in place.

7 Cut out a piece of thin card 7cm x 10cm.

8 Roll the card around the body under the arms and secure with sticky tape.

9 Draw on two eyes and a nose using the black felt tipped pen. Noah's beard will cover his mouth.

10 Cut out a rectangle of fabric 16cm x 6cm and fold in half.

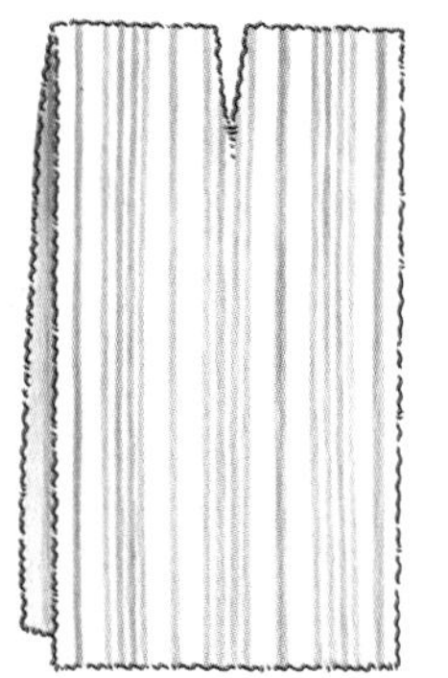

11 Cut a small slit across the fold, big enough to push the fabric down over the head.

12 Cut out a rectangle of fabric 14cm x 4cm. Cut a slit up the centre to half way and pass it over the head to make the overcoat.

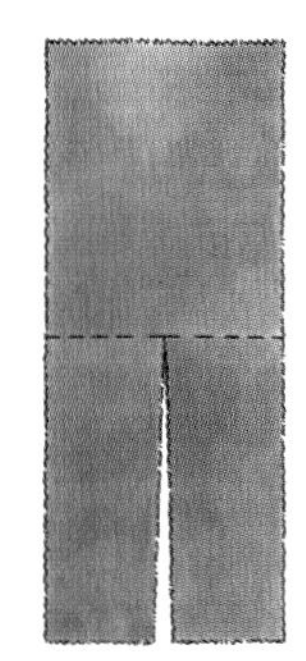

13 Tie around the waist with yarn to make a belt.

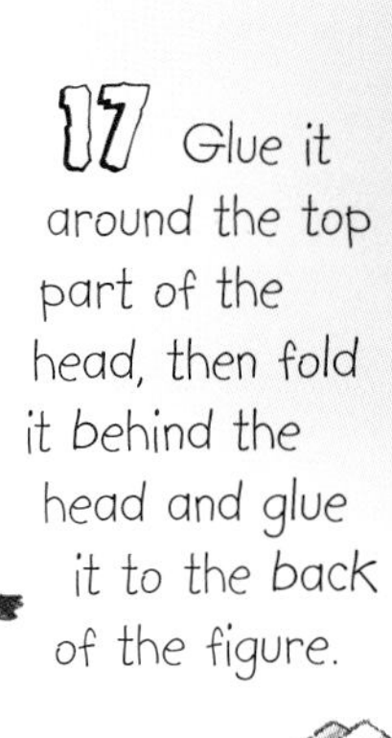

14 Thread the stick through the loop in Noah's hand.

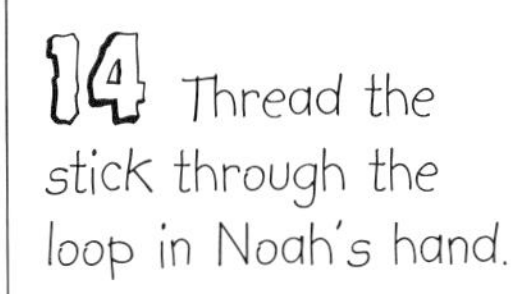

15 Make the beard with a small piece of white pipe cleaner. Push the ends into the top bead hole and glue the pipe cleaner around the face. Draw or paint on a white moustache.

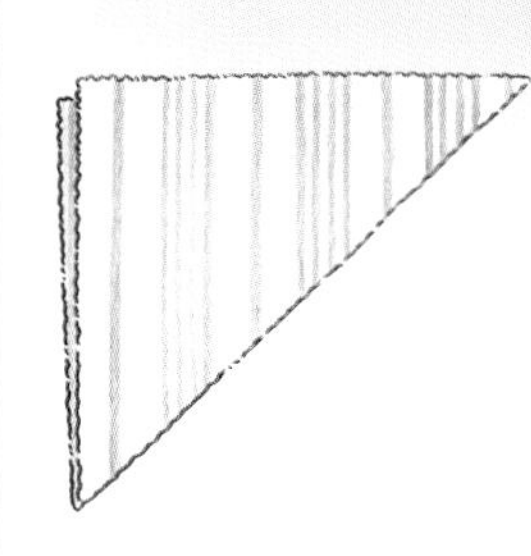

16 Cut out a square of fabric and fold it in half to make a triangle for the head-dress.

17 Glue it around the top part of the head, then fold it behind the head and glue it to the back of the figure.

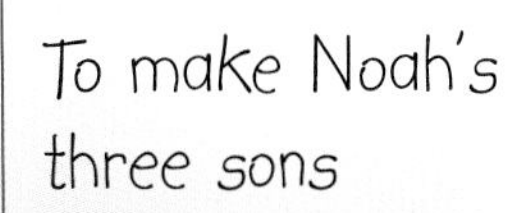

To make Noah's three sons

1 Follow the instructions for Noah, using different coloured fabrics for their clothes.

2 Draw on their moustaches with the black felt tipped pen and use brown or black pipe cleaners to make the beards.

To make Noah's wife and three daughters-in-law

1 Follow the instructions for Noah, using different coloured fabrics for their clothes but making no overcoats.

2 Draw on the faces but do not add beards!

This is what to do:

To make Noah's ark

'Find wood,' God said, 'and build an ark,
then paint it with hot tar.
Build rooms inside, put on the roof –
this ark will take you far!
Trust me – I will not let it sink.
Now store up plenty of food and drink.'

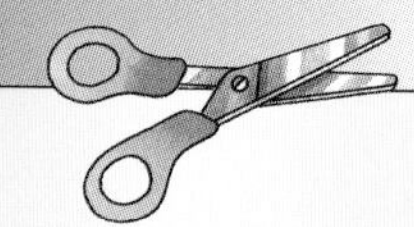

You will need:

Thin coloured card
Scissors
Sticky tape
Permanent ink black felt tipped pens
Pencil
Ruler
Poster paints and brush
Large shoebox
Paper fasteners
PVA glue in bottle with nozzle
Wooden craft sticks or ice-lolly sticks
Thick card
Pair of compasses
Craft knife and cutting mat, and some adult help with the cutting
Gravel, sand and small stones
Green and brown yarn
Empty cotton reels

Extra Tip: Wooden craft sticks can be easily cut with scissors

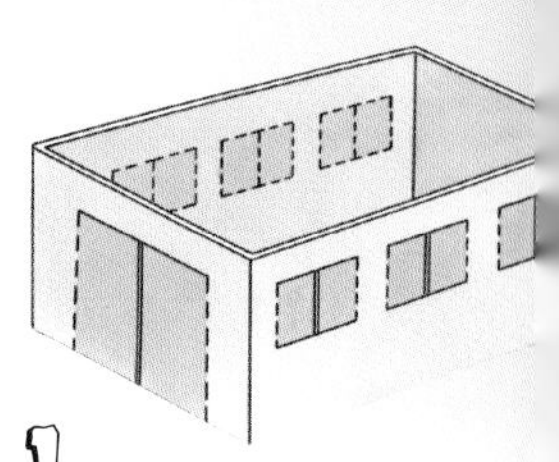

1
Use the pencil and ruler to draw the door on one end and three windows on each side of the shoebox.

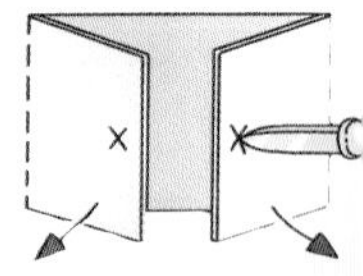

2
Ask an adult to help you cut along the pencil lines, then fold back each side of the windows and door to make the openings. Fix a paper fastener to each window and door to make the handles.

3
Paint the shoebox lid and leave to dry.

4 Cut a piece of card for the roof approximately 6cm longer and wider than the shoebox lid.

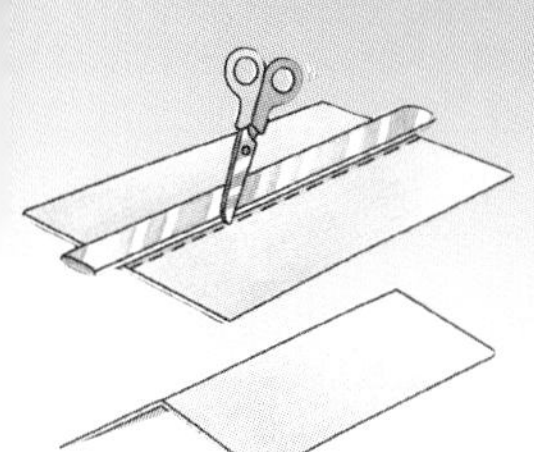

5 Draw a line half way across the card down the length of it. Ask an adult to help you score along the line using the blade of the scissors and bend the card to make the roof shape.

6 Cut a prop for the roof the same length as the shoebox lid and 8cm wide. Score and fold in half lengthways. Attach strips of sticky tape to the prop to keep the triangular shape.

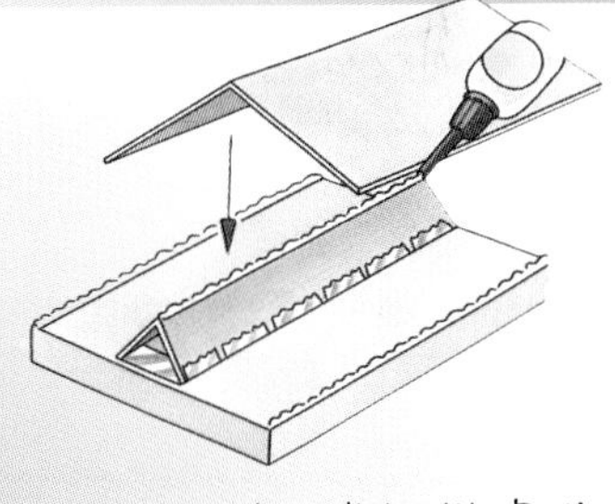

7 Glue the prop to the shoebox lid with PVA glue and then glue the roof on top of the lid.

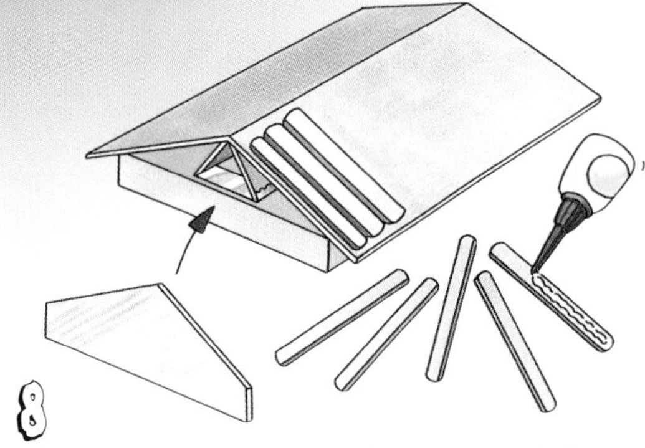

8 Glue the wooden craft sticks or ice lolly sticks to the roof. Cut out two triangular card shapes to cover the ends of the roof. Paint the shapes before gluing in place.

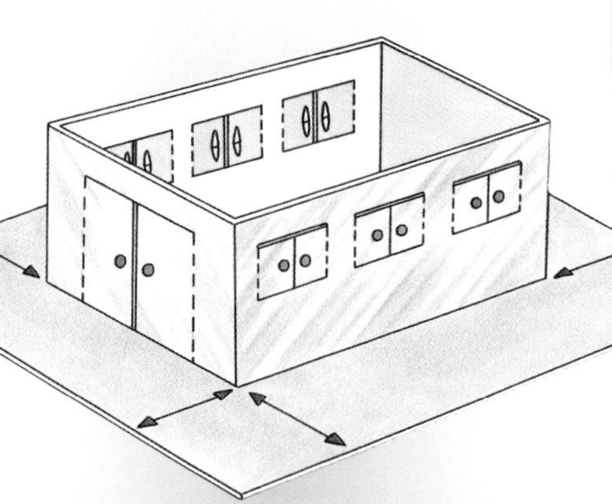

9 Cut a large piece of card approximately 20cm longer and 20cm wider than the shoe box to make the deck tray.

Measure a 3cm line around the card. Cut out the corners and score along the lines, then fold up the sides to make the deck tray. Secure the corners with sticky tape.

10 Cut out two boat shapes to cover the sides of the tray. Make them approximately 8cm high and longer than the sides, with curved ends. Cut a gap out of one of the sides for the ramp. Glue wooden craft sticks or ice lolly sticks over the shapes and leave to dry.

11 Paint the deck and glue the two sides in place. Glue the house part of the ark to the deck.

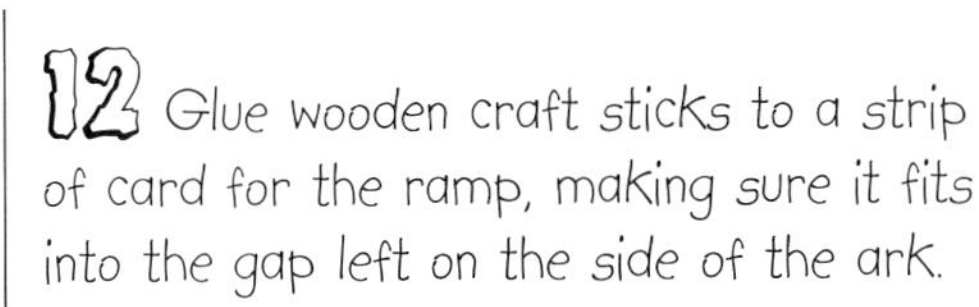

12 Glue wooden craft sticks to a strip of card for the ramp, making sure it fits into the gap left on the side of the ark.

This is what to do:

To make the donkey, horse and zebra

'There's one more thing,'
God said to Noah.
'Here's a big task for you:
fill the ark with every creature,
line them up two by two.'
Noah found donkeys,
and zebras with stripes,
mules and horses of different types.

You will need:

- Long 'craft' pipe cleaners
- Brown, grey, black and white yarn
- Small wooden beads, 18mm long
- Dark coloured bead for the zebra
- Scissors
- PVA glue in bottle with nozzle
- White poster paint and brush
- Sticky tape
- Permanent ink black felt tipped pen

To make the horses

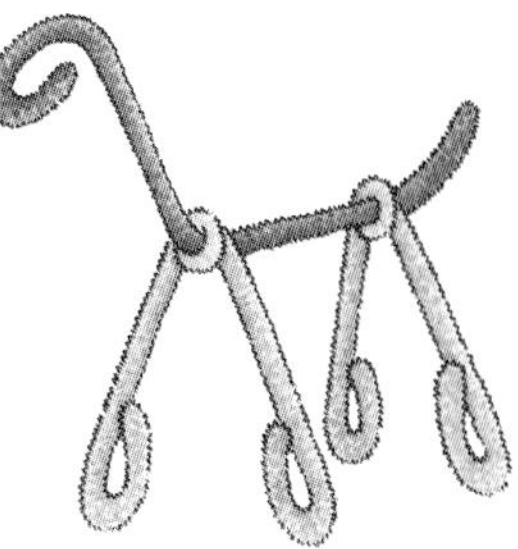

1 Bend a brown pipe cleaner to make the head and body shape and twist two more pipe cleaners around the body to make two pairs of legs. If the pipe cleaners are too long, cut them to size with scissors.

2 Twist a smaller piece of pipe cleaner around the head to make the ears.

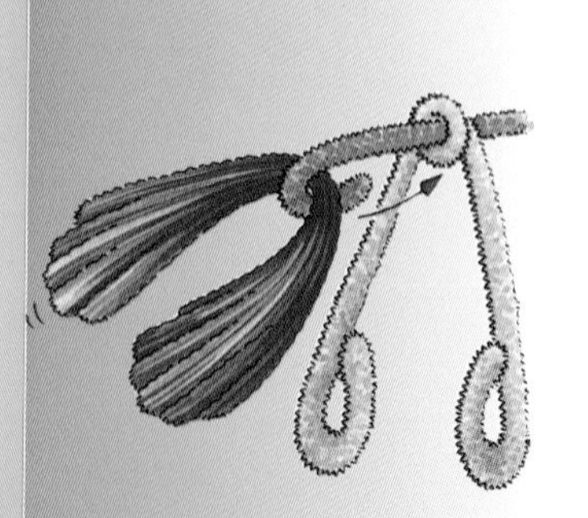

3 Cut several pieces of brown yarn for the tail and attach them to the rear end of the horse by looping them through the body pipe cleaner.

4 Glue a bead on to the neck to make the head, making sure the end of the pipe cleaner shows through the bead hole to make the nose.

5 Draw two eyes on to the bead with the felt tipped pen.

6 Wind brown yarn around the legs, body, neck and ears to cover the pipe cleaners, tucking the ends under and gluing over the joins.

7 Repeat to make the female horse.

To make the donkeys

1 Follow the instructions for the horse, but use grey pipe cleaners, make the legs shorter and the ears longer. Use grey yarn for the tail.

2 Wind grey yarn around the legs, body, neck and ears to cover the pipe cleaners, and wind more around the body to make it fatter.

3 Repeat to make the female donkey.

To make the zebras

1 Follow the instructions for the horse, but use black pipe cleaners and make the legs shorter.

2 Cut several pieces of black and white yarn for the tail and attach them to the rear end of the zebra by looping them through the body pipe cleaner.

3 Wind black yarn around the legs, body, neck and ears to cover the pipe cleaners.

4 Wind stripes of white yarn around the zebra's body and neck.

5 Glue a dark bead on to the neck to make the head, making sure the end of the pipe cleaner shows through the bead hole to make the nose, and paint on white eyes using the poster paint. When the paint is thoroughly dry, mark in the middle of the eyes with black felt tipped pen.

6 Repeat to make the female zebra.

This is what to do:

To make the sheep, dog, oxen and deer

Noah and his sons worked hard all week;
they had so many animals to find:
cows and bulls and deer and sheep,
male and female of every kind.
From fields and forests, bushes and trees,
fitting them in would be quite a squeeze!

You will need:

- Long 'craft' pipe cleaners, assorted colours
- Small wooden beads, 18mm long
- Small wooden beads, 6mm long
- Brown, beige, and white yarn
- Scissors
- PVA glue in bottle with nozzle
- Permanent ink black felt tipped pen

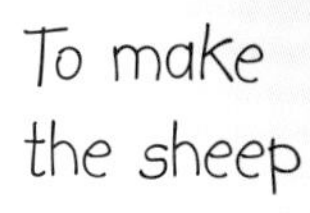

To make the sheep

1 Bend a black pipe cleaner to make the head and body shape and twist two smaller pieces of pipe cleaner around the body to make two pairs of legs.

2 Twist a smaller piece of pipe cleaner around the head to make the ears.

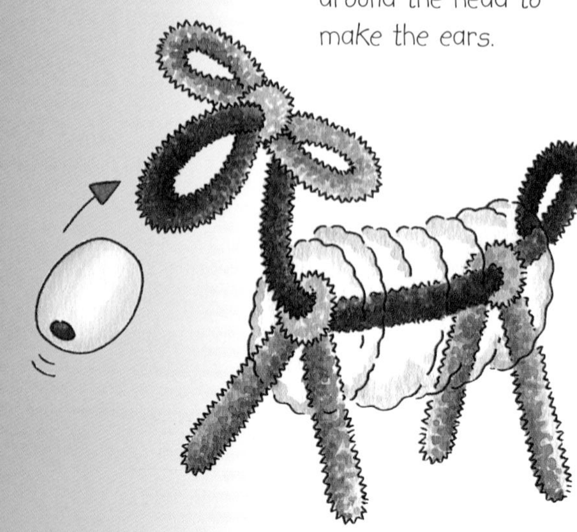

3 Glue a bead on to the neck to make the head, making sure the end of the pipe cleaner shows through the bead hole to make the nose.

4 Draw two eyes on to the bead with the felt tipped pen.

5 Wind thick white yarn around the legs, neck and ears to cover the pipe cleaners, and wind white yarn around the body making it fatter, tucking the ends under and gluing over the joins.

6 Repeat to make the female sheep.

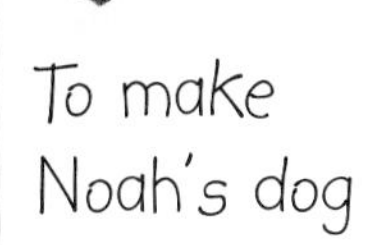

To make Noah's dog

1 Follow the instructions for the sheep, but use brown pipe cleaners and wind just enough brown yarn around the legs, body, neck and ears, to make it thinner.

To make the ox

1 Follow the instructions for the horse on pages 6-7, but bend the pipe cleaner into a loop to make the tail.

2 Give the ox shorter ears than the horse and twist a small piece of white pipe cleaner around the head to make the horns.

3 Glue a bead on to the pipe cleaner neck to make the head, making sure the end of the pipe cleaner shows through the bead hole to make the nose.

4 Draw on two eyes using the felt tipped pen.

5 Wind brown yarn around the legs, neck, ears and tail to cover the pipe cleaners. Then wind extra yarn around the body to make the ox fatter!

6 Repeat to make the female ox.

To make the deer

1 Follow the instructions for the horse on pages 6-7, but use white pipe cleaners and tuck the rear end pipe cleaner under the body, as deer do not have flowing tails. Wrap beige yarn around the deer.

2 Twist a brown pipe cleaner into the curly shape shown here to make the antlers for the stag, then twist them around the head to attach them.

3 Repeat to make the female deer, but make tiny horns out of very small beads instead of antlers.

This is what to do:

To make the camels, giraffes and elephants

God wanted Noah to gather the animals
and keep them safe in the ark:
trumpeting elephants, raging rhinos,
and hedgehogs that hunt in the dark;
spitting camels with one or two humps,
long-necked giraffes might have a few bumps!

You will need:

Long 'craft' pipe cleaners, assorted colours

Small wooden beads, 18mm long

Larger wooden beads for the elephants' heads

Small wooden beads, 6mm long, for the giraffes' horns

Cotton wool balls

Brown, grey and yellow yarn

Scissors

PVA glue in bottle with nozzle

Permanent ink black felt tipped pen

Grey felt

To make the camel

1 Follow the instructions for the horse on pages 6-7, but and make the neck and the legs longer and leave a length of pipe cleaner for the tail.

2 Add in an extra piece of pipe cleaner to make the hump shape. Secure the ends of the hump where the legs twist around the body.

3 Twist a smaller piece of pipe cleaner around the head to make the ears. Glue a bead on to the neck to make the head.

4 Draw on two eyes using the felt tipped pen.

5 Wind brown yarn around the legs, neck and ears to cover the pipe cleaners, tucking the ends under and gluing over the joins.

6 Pad out the hump with a cotton wool ball and wind brown yarn around the body and tail.

7 Repeat to make the female camel.

To make the giraffe

1 Follow the instructions for the horse on pages 6-7, but use yellow pipe cleaners and make the neck much longer, so the giraffe is taller than the camel. Wrap yellow yarn around the giraffe.

2 Twist a small piece of pipe cleaner around the head and attach the very small beads to each end to make the giraffe's small horns.

3 Decorate the giraffe with spots using a black felt tipped pen.

4 Repeat to make the female giraffe.

To make the elephant

1 Bend a grey pipe cleaner to make the body shape making the neck extra long so that it extends into the trunk. Twist two more pipe cleaners around the body to make two pairs of legs.

2 Glue a large bead on to the neck to make the head. Push the pipe cleaner through the bead hole to make the trunk and twist a small piece of white pipe cleaner around the base of the trunk for the tusks.

3 Draw on two eyes with the black felt tipped pen.

4 Wind thick grey yarn around the legs, tail, neck and trunk to cover the pipe cleaners, tucking the ends under and gluing over the joins.

5 Pad out the body with cotton wool balls to make it fatter before winding the grey yarn around the body.

6 Cut a pair of ears from the grey felt and glue them to the head.

7 Repeat to make the female elephant but make her tusks smaller.

This is what to do:

To make the lions, tigers and leopards

In the beginning God had filled the world with beautiful, wonderful creatures.
He wanted Noah to keep them safe, with their colourful camouflage features:
tigers with stripes and powerful paws,
leopards with spots, and the lion that roars.

You will need:

Long 'craft' pipe cleaners, assorted colours

Small wooden beads, 20mm long

Cotton wool balls

Black, orange and yellow yarn

Black thread

Scissors

PVA glue in bottle with nozzle

Permanent ink black felt tipped pen

To make the lioness

1 Follow the instructions for the horse on pages 6-7, but use yellow pipe cleaners, make the neck and legs shorter, and leave a length of pipe cleaner for the tail.

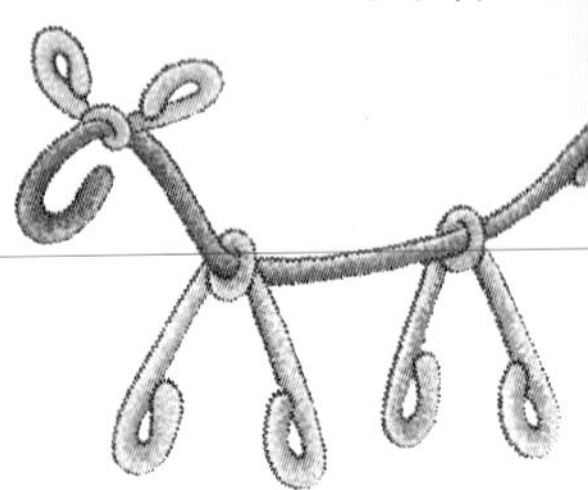

2 Use a large round bead for the head and push it on to the neck, making sure a short piece of pipe cleaner sticks out.

3 Cut four short lengths of black thread and twist the pipe cleaner around them to make whiskers. Glue the head to the neck so the whiskers and the end of the pipe cleaner show through the bead hole.

4 Draw on two eyes with the black felt tipped pen.

5 Twist a small length of pipe cleaner around the head to make the ears.

6 Wind yellow yarn around the ears, neck, legs and tail to cover up the pipe cleaners, tucking the ends under and gluing over the joins.

7 Pad out the body with cotton wool balls to make it fatter, then wind the yellow yarn around the body.

8 Repeat to make the male lion, but twist a pipe cleaner into a circle that will fit around the bead head to make his mane, leaving the pipe cleaner ends at the top.

9 Wind yellow yarn around the circle until it is completely covered. Slot the ends of the pipe cleaner into the bead hole in the top of the lion's head and glue the mane in place around the face.

To make the tiger

1 Follow the instructions for the lioness but use orange pipe cleaners, and orange yarn to cover the pipe cleaner body, legs and tail.

2 Wind black yarn around the tiger's body and neck to give him stripes.

3 Repeat to make the female tiger.

To make the leopard

1 Follow the instructions for the lioness but decorate the leopard with spots using a black felt tipped pen.

2 Repeat to make the female elephant.

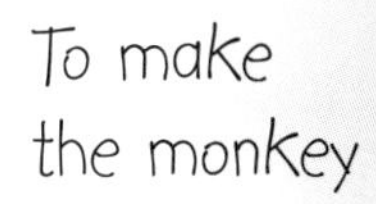

This is what to do:

To make the monkeys and kangaroos

God told Noah to feed the animals,
but what did they like to eat?
The chattering monkeys, the kangaroos
and the bears with padded feet.
Noah looked round at the world's first zoo:
hundreds of animals, two by two.

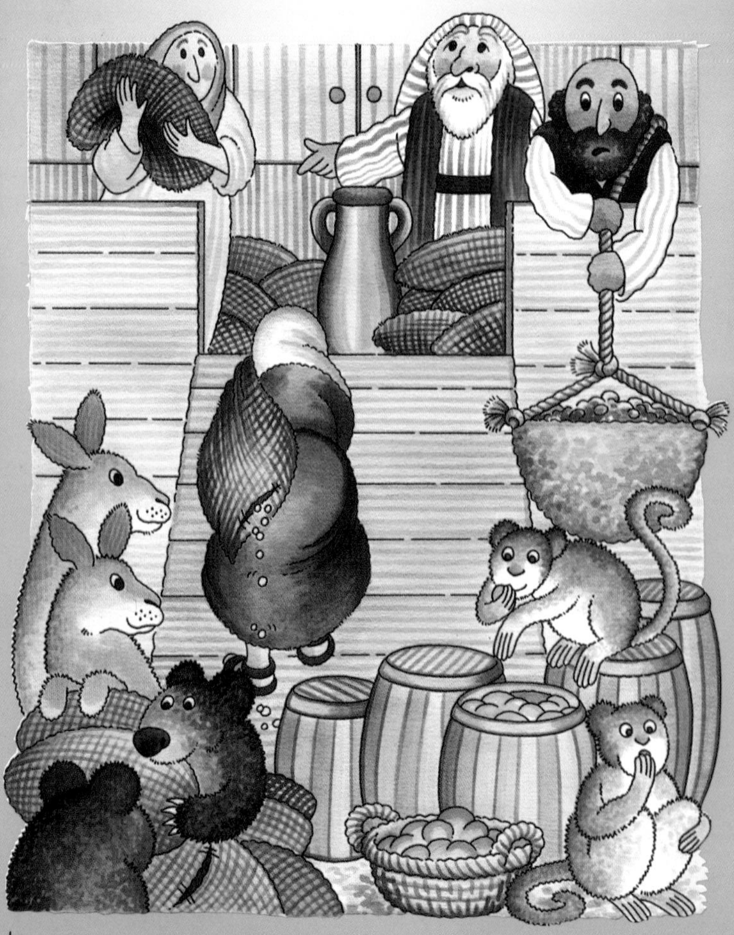

You will need:

- Long 'craft' pipe cleaners, assorted colours
- Small wooden beads, 18mm long
- Small wooden beads, 12.5mm long for the baby kangaroo's head
- Cotton wool balls
- Brown, blue, and grey yarn
- Scissors
- PVA glue in bottle with nozzle
- Permanent ink black felt tipped pen
- Small scraps of brown and grey felt

To make the monkey

1 Bend a grey pipe cleaner to make the head and body shape and leave a long length of pipe cleaner for the tail. Twist two more pipe cleaners around the body to make the arms and legs.

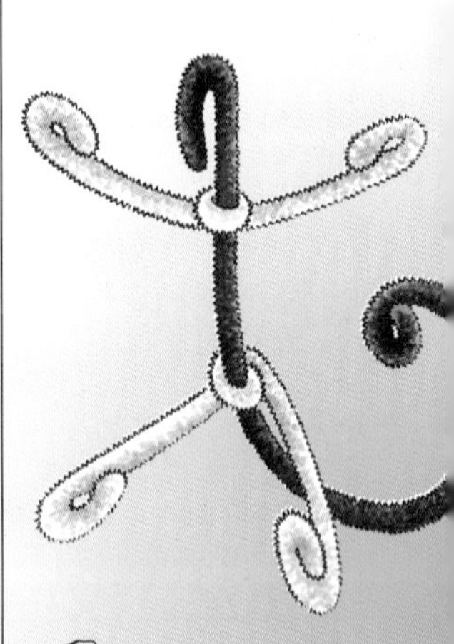

2 Glue a bead on to the neck to make the head.

3 Draw on the eyes, nose and mouth with the felt tipped pen.

4 Wind grey and blue yarn around the arms, legs, body and tail to cover the pipe cleaners. Wind extra yarn around the body to make it fatter. Finish off the ends of the yarn by tucking them under and gluing over the joins.

5 Cut out two small ear shapes from the felt and glue them to each side of the head.

6 Repeat to make the female monkey but use brown yarn.

To make the Kangaroo

1 Bend a brown pipe cleaner to make the head and body shape and leave a long length of pipe cleaner for the tail. Twist two more pipe cleaners around the body to make the arms and legs.

2 Twist a small piece of pipe cleaner around the head to make the ears. Glue a bead on to the neck to make the head.

3 Draw on the eyes with the felt tipped pen.

4 Wind brown yarn around the arms, legs, ears and tail to cover the pipe cleaners.

5 Pad out the body with cotton wool balls to give it the kangaroo shape, before winding yarn around the body.

6 Repeat to make the female kangaroo.

7 Bend the pipe cleaner into the shape shown here to make the joey and attach a very small bead for the head. Wind brown yarn around the ears.

8 Attach the baby to the female's body by winding yarn around until the pipe cleaner neck is covered.

This is what to do:

To make crocodiles, turtles and snakes

Now all the animals were on board,
it was time for the reptile and snake,
and crocodiles snapping their jaws –
was this a big mistake?
A boa constrictor might eat the goat;
the slow old tortoise nearly missed the boat.

You will need:

Long 'craft' pipe cleaners, assorted colours

Small wooden beads, 18mm long

Small wooden beads, 6mm long

Large wooden bead, 20mm long

Cotton wool balls

Brown and green yarn

Scissors

PVA glue and cocktail sticks

Permanent ink black felt tipped pen

Coloured thread

Extra Tip: when gluing tiny things, put a small amount of glue in a plastic lid and use a cocktail stick to dab small blobs of glue where you need it!

To make the crocodile

1 Bend a green pipe cleaner to make the head and body shape and leave a long length of pipe cleaner at each end for the head and tail. Twist two more pipe cleaners around the body to make the pairs of legs.

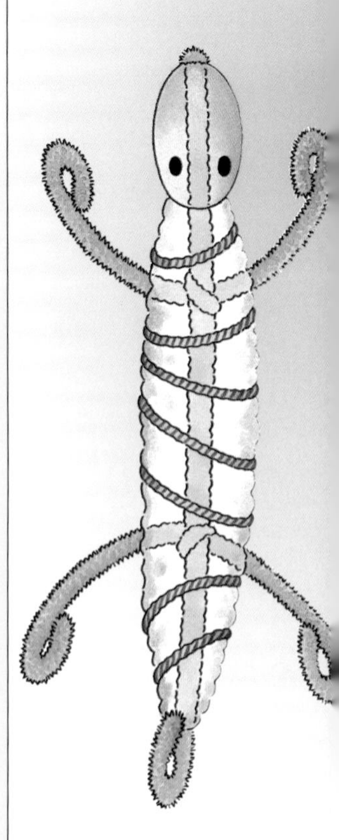

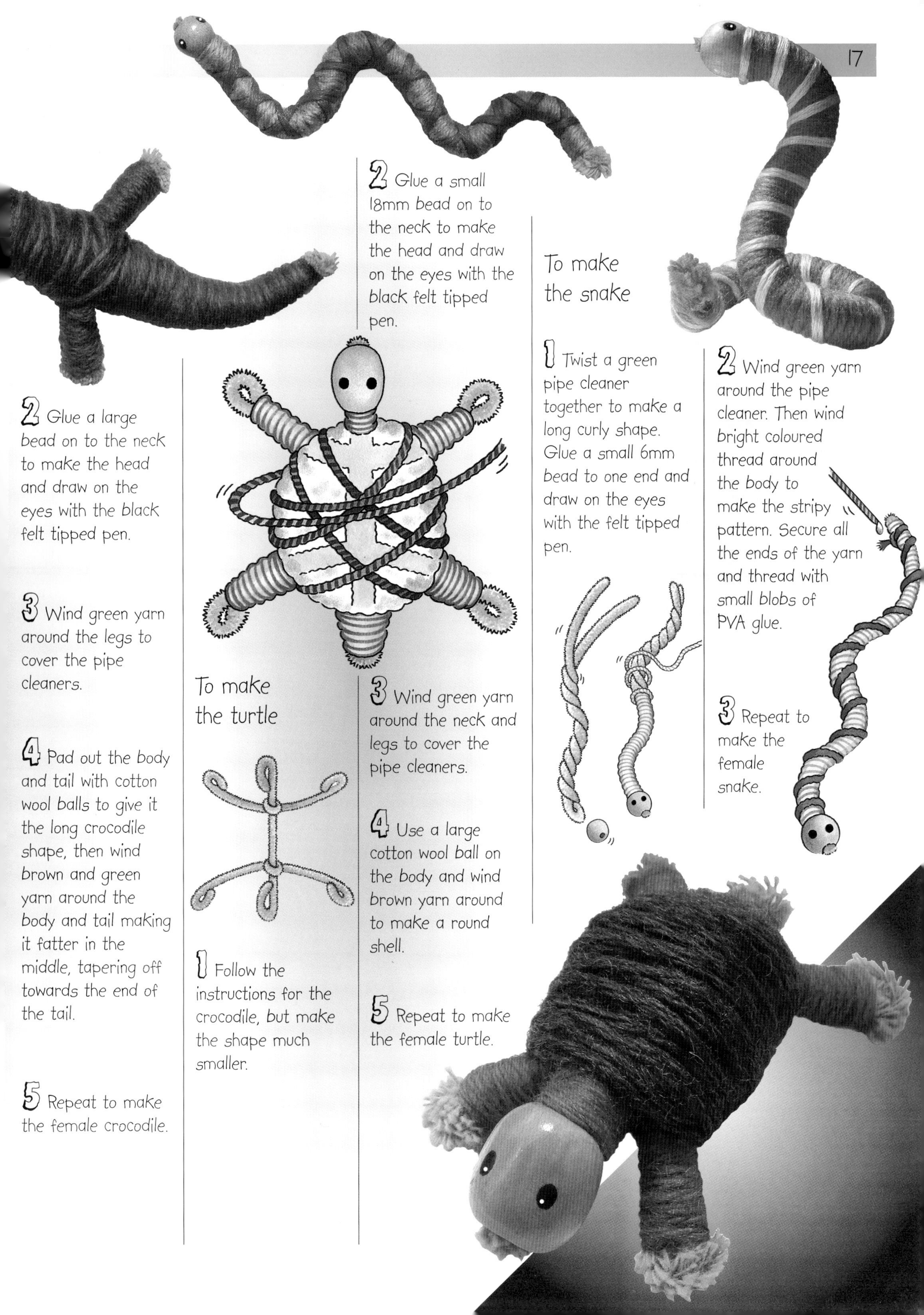

2 Glue a large bead on to the neck to make the head and draw on the eyes with the black felt tipped pen.

3 Wind green yarn around the legs to cover the pipe cleaners.

4 Pad out the body and tail with cotton wool balls to give it the long crocodile shape, then wind brown and green yarn around the body and tail making it fatter in the middle, tapering off towards the end of the tail.

5 Repeat to make the female crocodile.

To make the turtle

1 Follow the instructions for the crocodile, but make the shape much smaller.

2 Glue a small 18mm bead on to the neck to make the head and draw on the eyes with the black felt tipped pen.

3 Wind green yarn around the neck and legs to cover the pipe cleaners.

4 Use a large cotton wool ball on the body and wind brown yarn around to make a round shell.

5 Repeat to make the female turtle.

To make the snake

1 Twist a green pipe cleaner together to make a long curly shape. Glue a small 6mm bead to one end and draw on the eyes with the felt tipped pen.

2 Wind green yarn around the pipe cleaner. Then wind bright coloured thread around the body to make the stripy pattern. Secure all the ends of the yarn and thread with small blobs of PVA glue.

3 Repeat to make the female snake.

This is what to do:

To make the peacocks and flamingos

'Phew!' thought Noah.
'We're nearly ready.
There's no room for any more!'
But fluttering, chattering,
squawking and strutting,
the birds came through the door!
The pink flamingo, the peacock proud;
Noah mopped his brow: what a noisy crowd!

You will need:

- Long 'craft' pipe cleaners, assorted colours
- Small wooden beads, 18mm long
- Small wooden beads, 12.5mm long
- Green, blue and pink yarn
- Stiff card
- Round coloured stickers
- Scissors
- PVA glue
- Permanent ink black felt tipped pen

To make the peacock

1 Cut out a semi-circular piece of stiff card approximately 5cm in diameter. Ask an adult to help make a hole in the card and cut notches around the curved edge as illustrated.

2 Wind coloured yarn around the card, starting with a length of turquoise, then blue and green, and build up the fan-shaped tail pattern. Tuck the ends of the yarn underneath the winding when finishing, and secure all ends with dabs of PVA.

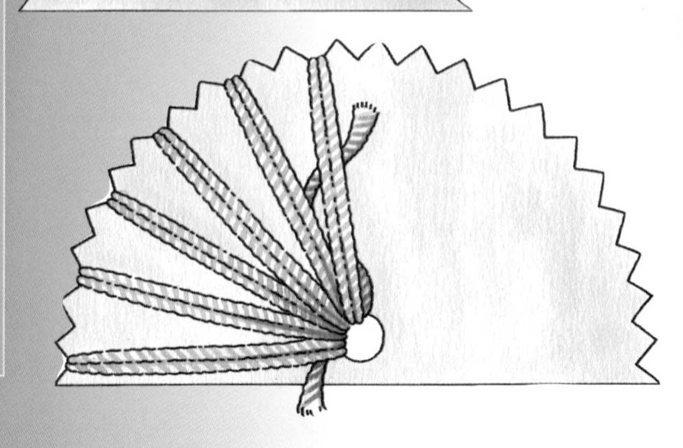

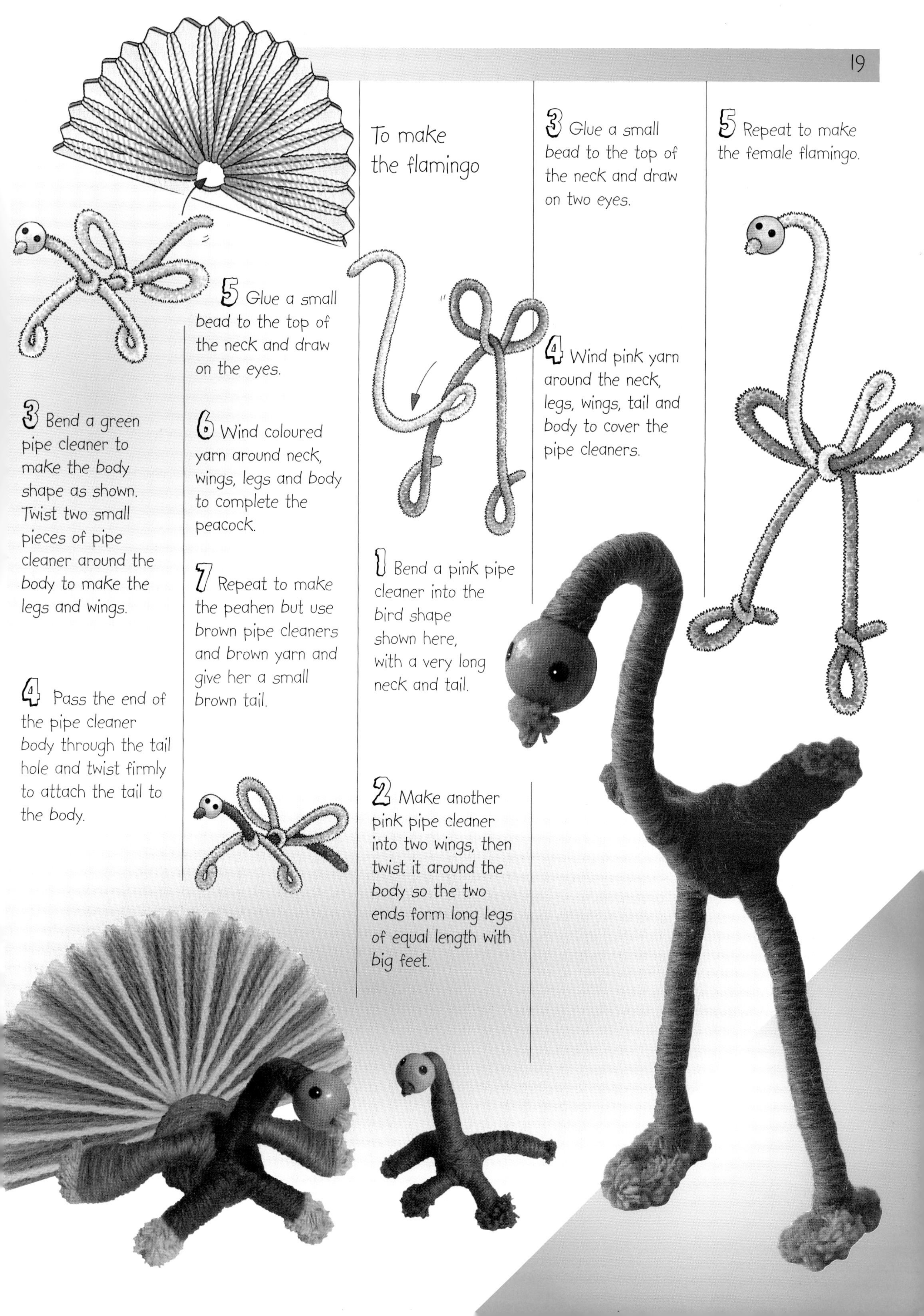

3 Bend a green pipe cleaner to make the body shape as shown. Twist two small pieces of pipe cleaner around the body to make the legs and wings.

4 Pass the end of the pipe cleaner body through the tail hole and twist firmly to attach the tail to the body.

5 Glue a small bead to the top of the neck and draw on the eyes.

6 Wind coloured yarn around neck, wings, legs and body to complete the peacock.

7 Repeat to make the peahen but use brown pipe cleaners and brown yarn and give her a small brown tail.

To make the flamingo

1 Bend a pink pipe cleaner into the bird shape shown here, with a very long neck and tail.

2 Make another pink pipe cleaner into two wings, then twist it around the body so the two ends form long legs of equal length with big feet.

3 Glue a small bead to the top of the neck and draw on two eyes.

4 Wind pink yarn around the neck, legs, wings, tail and body to cover the pipe cleaners.

5 Repeat to make the female flamingo.

This is what to do:

To make the ark at sea scene

God closed the door;

the rain poured down.

The floods reached the mountain-top.

Noah's dear wife and three sons kept saying,

'Just when will this rain stop?'

There was such a noise inside the ark:

Roar, miaow, moo, grunt, neigh, quack, bark!

You will need:

- Thick card
- Pair of compasses
- Holographic silver or gold card
- Scissors
- Craft knife and cutting mat, and some adult help with the cutting
- PVA glue
- Poster paints and brush
- Strips of dark and light blue tissue paper

To make the background

1 Ask an adult to help you use the compasses to draw a semi-circular arc on the card, then carefully cut it out. Paint the card with a dark, stormy sky.

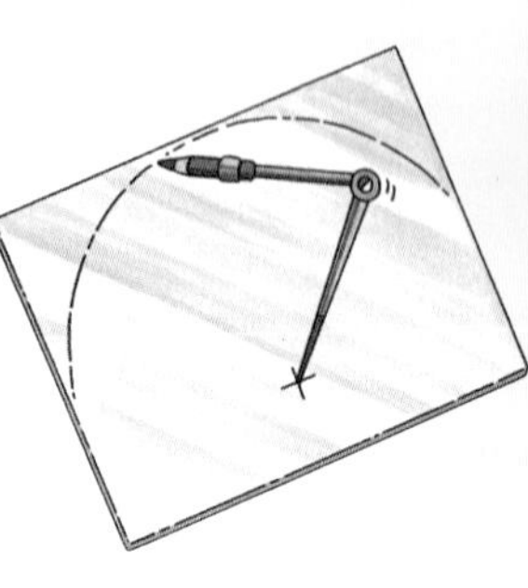

2 Draw some cloud-shapes on the card. Cut them out and paint them.

3 Glue small pieces of thick card to the backs of the clouds. This will give them a 3-dimensional look when you glue them to the sky.

4 Draw some lightning flashes on the holographic card and cut them out.

5 Position the clouds on the backdrop and glue them in place with PVA glue.

6 Glue the lightning flashes to the sky so they look as if they are flashing from under the clouds.

To make the scene

1 Position the ark on a table-top and prop the stormy backdrop behind the ark.

2 Use the strands of blue tissue paper to create a stormy sea effect around the ark.

3 Place Noah, his wife and family on the deck of the ark and surround them with all the animals you have made. Position some animals on the roof and peeping out of the windows.

This is what to do:

To make the ark scene with the rainbow

After many long weeks
the waters went down.
Noah thanked God and shouted, 'Hurray!'
Out trooped the animals, two by two,
and God made a rainbow to say:
'Never again will I flood these lands.'
Noah and his ark had been safe
in God's hands.

You will need:

- Thick card
- Pair of compasses
- Scissors
- Craft knife and cutting mat, and some adult help with the cutting
- PVA glue
- Poster paints and brush
- Gravel, sand and small stones
- Pipe cleaners
- Green and brown yarn
- Empty cotton reels
- Pencil with sharp point
- Brown paper

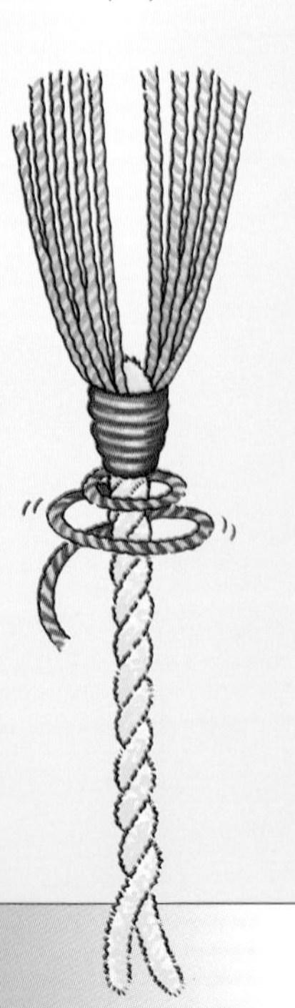

To make the trees

1. Cut the green yarn into 12cm lengths.
2. Twist a pipe cleaner around the lengths of yarn to secure them. Continue twisting the pipe cleaner to make the tree trunk.

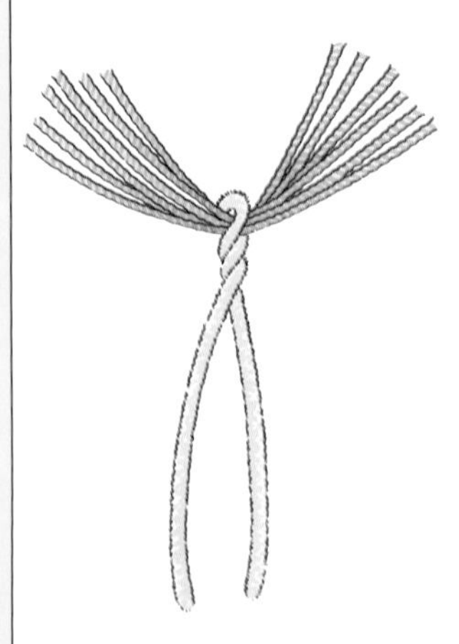

3. Cover the pipe cleaner with lengths of brown yarn, wrapping it around the trunk and gluing it in place.

4 Cover the cotton reel with brown yarn, gluing it to the reel with PVA glue. Cover the top of the reel with a disc of brown paper, making the centre hole with a pencil point.

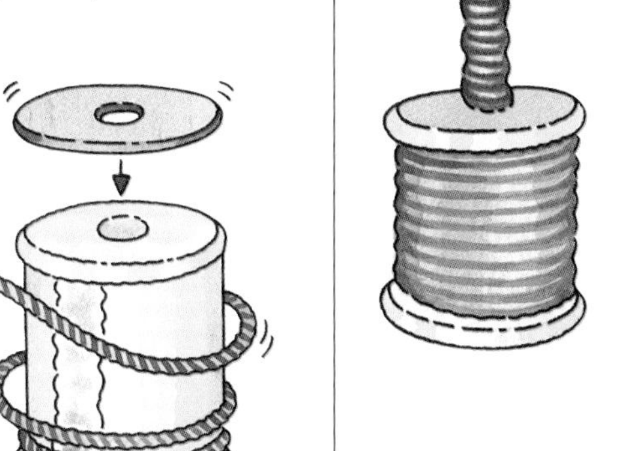

5 Glue the tree trunk into the cotton reel.

6 Repeat to make lots of trees, but make them different heights, and use different coloured yarns.

To make the background

1 Ask an adult to help you use the compasses to draw a semi-circular arc on the card just like the stormy backdrop, then carefully cut it out.

2 Using the same circle centre, use the compasses again to mark out the rainbow shape on the card.

3 Paint the backdrop making the sky bright blue. Be very careful when you paint the rainbow to get the colours in the right order. Starting from the bottom they are violet, indigo, blue, green, yellow, orange and red.

To make the scene

1 Position the ark on a table top with the ramp in place at the side. Prop the rainbow backdrop behind the ark.

2 Use the sand, gravel and stones to create the effect of dry land around the ark and put the trees in place.

3 Place Noah and his family by the ramp unloading the ark and show the animals coming out, two by two.

Published in the UK by

The Bible Reading Fellowship

First Floor, Elsfield Hall,
15-17 Elsfield Way, Oxford OX2 8FG

ISBN 1 84101 397 8

First edition 2004

Editorial Director Annette Reynolds

Project Editor Leena Lane

Art Director Gerald Rogers

Pre-production Krystyna Hewitt

Production John Laister

British Library Cataloguing in Publication Data.

A catalogue record for this book is available from the British Library.

Printed and bound in Singapore

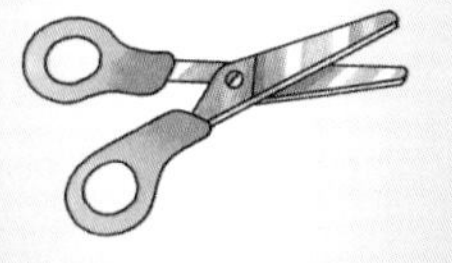